TAKE COURAGE

60 DAYS FOR

CWR

Published 2016 by CWR, Waverley Abbey House, Waverley Lane, Farnham, Surrey GU9 8EP, UK. CWR is a Registered Charity – Number 294387 and a Limited Company registered in England – Registration Number 1990308.

For list of National Distributors, visit www.cwr.org.uk/distributors

Text adapted from parts of *YP's* issues: November/December 2013, September/October 2014, November/December 2014.
Concept development, editing, design and production by CWR
Printed in the UK by Linney Group.
ISBN: 978-1-78259-519-9

CONTENTS

COURAGE

INTRO

Take courage. Seriously, take it! We all need it, but we all lack it from time to time (or, if we admit it, probably most of the time!).

Why is this book called *Take Courage*? Well, we've got three main themes to look at. First up in **ARE YOU LISTENING?**, we look at **prayer** and how we communicate with God, who created us and created courage in the first place. And He will give it to us in abundance through His Holy Spirit.

Next in **GIVE IT SOME HEART** we look at the life of **David** – a young lad who needed incredible courage to stand up to Goliath, and who needed courage all the way through the rest of his life too.

Lastly we face up to **doubt** and how we can overcome it in **DOUBT-BUSTERS**. We need courage to face up to our fears and stand up to those who doubt our faith or try to persuade us to accept less than the best.

So there you have it. We hope you enjoy what's within these pages, and that it gives you the courage you need for whatever situation you're facing.

'Be on your guard; stand firm in the faith; be courageous; be strong' **1 Corinthians 16:13**

ARE YOU LISTENING?

IT'S GOOD TO TALK

'pray in the Spirit on all occasions with all kinds of prayers and requests. With this in mind, be alert and always keep on praying for all the Lord's people. Pray also for me, that whenever I speak, words may be given me so that I will fearlessly make known the mystery of the gospel, for which I am an ambassador in chains. Pray that I may declare it fearlessly, as I should.'

Ephesians 6:18–20

Question: What's the most exciting, dynamic, exhilarating, mind-blowing thing in the universe?

Answer: Spending time talking and listening to God – otherwise known as ... prayer! OK, so you may not always feel that way, but prayer is a chance to express ourselves to God. And it's also a chance for God to express Himself to us. Yeah, it's a two-way thing, a back-and-forth exchange between us and our Creator.

At some point in your life you've probably heard the phrase, 'It's good to talk'. Why is it so good? Because talking lets us **EXPRESS OURSELVES** and helps us get closer to other people.

If there's something on your mind and there's no one to talk it through with, it can make life very difficult.

On the other hand, if you're really happy about something and there's no one to get excited with, that can be really frustrating too! Expressing ourselves makes good times even better, and bad times just that little bit easier to handle. After all, as the old saying goes: a burden shared is a burden halved. If you have something really heavy to carry, it's much better to ask someone to help rather than try to struggle along on your own.

By far the best person to express ourselves to, and ask to share our burdens with, is God. Whatever's on our mind, we can talk to Him about it. It doesn't matter what we want to say, God loves to hear from us, **ANY TIME, ANY PLACE.** What's more, God doesn't just listen. He answers our prayers too.

Grab some paper and a pen and express yourself to God in words or pictures. Be as creative or as direct as you like!

EXPRESSION

HE'S THE BOSS

'"Indeed Herod and Pontius Pilate met together with the Gentiles and the people of Israel in this city to conspire against your holy servant Jesus, whom you anointed. They did what your power and will had decided beforehand should happen. Now, Lord, consider their threats and enable your servants to speak your word with great boldness. Stretch out your hand to heal and perform signs and wonders through the name of your holy servant Jesus." After they prayed, the place where they were meeting was shaken. And they were all filled with the Holy Spirit and spoke the word of God boldly.' **Acts 4:27–31**

It was a moving prayer meeting – the floor moved, the walls moved and the roof moved. Everyone was calm but the building was badly shaken.

Peter and John had been told by the Jewish religious leaders to stop talking about Jesus or get a one-way ticket to martyrdom. But they weren't shaken by their experience. Instead, they met with other Christians to talk to God about the situation. That was a good start.

It was the same as saying, 'Lord, You are the boss, You are in control of the situation ...' **THEY HAD THE CREATOR OF THE UNIVERSE ON THEIR SIDE,** so why worry about a few trumped up men in fancy robes?

And they didn't ask for an opt-out clause on witnessing. Or for God to zap their enemies. They asked God for the power to obey and tell the world about Jesus. God heard, answered their request and dispatched the power they needed – so much power it nearly brought the house down.

>ENGAGE

God is in charge and He has the power to change people and situations. In prayer, you can express yourself to the Creator of the universe. Nothing is impossible. Ask yourself: what does God want me to do today? Then go for it! God will always give you the power to obey Him. So why not ask Him to help you live for Him today?

POWER

RELAY

'the Spirit helps us in our weakness. We do not know what we ought to pray for, but the Spirit himself intercedes for us through wordless groans. And he who searches our hearts knows the mind of the Spirit, because the Spirit intercedes for God's people in accordance with the will of God.' **Romans 8:26–27**

Us guys sometimes don't like to talk too much, but being shy or tongue-tied is never an excuse not to talk to God. Especially when you have someone to help you …

If praying is a chance to express ourselves to God and praying really can shake the world, why don't we pray? (Good question, eh?) Perhaps we don't believe our prayers make a difference (after all, it's only little old me!). Or is it because we don't know how to strike up a conversation with God?

No problem! God knows how helpless we feel at times. And ***HE UNDERSTANDS*** that we don't always know what to say and how to say it. That's why the Holy Spirit helps us when we pray.

We may think our prayers are mumbling messages far too embarrassing to let others hear. But our prayers are relayed to God through the Holy Spirit. And the Holy Spirit lets God know what we really want to say to Him.

Today's reading shows us that the Holy Spirit expresses the true meaning of our prayers to God on our behalf. He's there for us when words are not enough.

Do you believe your prayers make a difference? With the Holy Spirit, you can be sure that they do.

PRAY

Lord, I don't always find it easy to pray. I thank You that You have given me the Holy Spirit, who puts the power into my prayers. Help me to listen to Him when I pray. In Jesus' name. Amen.

SPIRIT

WHO ME?

'Then God said, "Let us make mankind in our image, in our likeness, so that they may rule over the fish in the sea and the birds in the sky, over the livestock and all the wild animals, and over all the creatures that move along the ground." So God created mankind in his own image, in the image of God he created them; male and female he created them.'

Genesis 1:26–27

Why does God, who is **ALL-POWERFUL AND ALL-KNOWING** (and we promise you He is), want us to talk to Him? After all, He already knows all about us. Good question, eh? To answer it, we need to get back to basics. And a good place to start is right back at the very beginning, in the book of Genesis (which means 'origin' or 'formation' and is the name of the first book of the Bible).

God didn't make us to jump at the touch of a button. He made people in His image and gave them the responsibility of ruling over the earth. Right at the start God said, 'It's over to you …'

Do you understand what this means? We are **CO-WORKERS OR PARTNERS WITH GOD.** He wants to carry out His plans through us. He created us so we could communicate with Him.

God lets us choose how we are going to live. We can do our own thing and ignore Him completely, because He never forces Himself into our lives. Or we can become His partners and live our lives with Him in control, which is when prayer becomes so important.

Are you ready to start really living *with* God and *for* Him?

PRAY

Father, Thank You for creating me. Help me to talk to You and to use my abilities in a way You want. Amen.

PARTNERS

IN THE IMAGE

'You have made them a little lower than the angels and crowned them with glory and honour. You made them rulers over the works of your hands; you put everything under their feet: all flocks and herds, and the animals of the wild, the birds in the sky, and the fish in the sea, all that swim the paths of the seas ... The highest heavens belong to the LORD, but the earth he has given to the human race.' **Psalm 8:5–8; 115:16**

Have you ever been told you look like someone else? It's the kind of thing relatives say without realising that just makes you cringe: 'You are getting to look more like your father each day.' Well, we were all made to remind people of someone else. But who?

We were made in the image of God, **CROWNED WITH GLORY.** When the rest of creation saw Adam, they saw a reflection of God. Just as the moon has no light of its own but reflects the light from the sun, Adam was simply reflecting God. And he kept in close contact with God so he could **RULE THE EARTH** as God wanted.

So, if people have authority to run the world and are a reflection of God to the rest of creation, what has gone wrong? Basically, Adam disobeyed God, the relationship was broken and our world is running without the Maker's instructions.

Being in God's family, we have His Spirit at work in us. The more time we spend with God, through prayer, and the more the fruit of the Spirit is seen in our lives, the more we will reflect His glory.

PRAY

Father God, I want people to look at me and see a reflection of You. I want to reflect and represent Your glory to those around me. Help me remember this. Amen.

THE GOOD NEWS AND THE BAD NEWS

'The devil led him up to a high place and showed him in an instant all the kingdoms of the world. And he said to him, "I will give you all their authority and splendour; it has been given to me, and I can give it to anyone I want to. If you worship me, it will all be yours." Jesus answered, "It is written: 'Worship the Lord your God and serve him only.'"' **Luke 4:5–8**

Do you want to hear the good news first or the bad news?

The good news is that God put us in charge of our world. The bad news is that we have handed control over to God's enemy. Lets take a further look ...

The good news ...

Right at the start, God gave us ***THE RIGHT TO RULE OUR WORLD.*** Wow, that's what I call authority! But we were also given the right to give that authority away.

The bad news ...

Satan wanted to rule the world: so who did he mislead? Who handed him the power to be in charge? It certainly wasn't Jesus, who refused to hand power or authority to Satan! It was Adam! As human beings we disobeyed God and surrendered His authority to Satan.

But wait ... there's more good news!
GOD HAD A SOLUTION – one which cost Him His own Son (Heb. 2:14). To give the authority on earth back to man, God became man – the Lord Jesus Christ. Jesus came to give us back our original position and status in creation. And because of Jesus we can become God's friends, His partners. God and us together.

Through our prayers, God's plans can become reality on planet Earth. Are you getting excited?

PRAY

Dear Jesus, teach me how to pray, so that Your will might be done on earth as it is in heaven. Amen.

BREAK-THROUGH

'After a long time, in the third year, the word of the LORD came to Elijah: "Go and present yourself to Ahab, and I will send rain on the land." So Elijah went to present himself to Ahab. Now the famine was severe in Samaria, and Ahab had summoned Obadiah, his palace administrator. (Obadiah was a devout believer in the LORD. While Jezebel was killing off the LORD's prophets, Obadiah had taken a hundred prophets and hidden them in two caves, fifty in each, and had supplied them with food and water.)'

1 Kings 18:1–4

Here we have Elijah, the faith-filled Old Testament hero chosen by God to pull wayward Israel back from the brink. Three-and-a-half parched years have passed without a drop of rain. Then comes the breakthrough – God tells Elijah He is going to send rain.

But before Elijah gets out his umbrella, there's some pretty intense action. The famous showdown on Mount Carmel takes place: 450 bad guys lined up against Elijah and God. They rave around their altar but their false god doesn't respond (and they get cut up about it).

Elijah prays, then God barbecues his offering and **THE BAD GUYS GET WIPED OUT.** But still no rain … God said it would rain.

Elijah gives a weather forecast. Clear blue skies turning to heavy rain. Then he prays. But there is not a cloud in the sky. Can't these weather forecasters ever get it right? He prays a second … third … fourth time. Not a hint of a cloud. He keeps praying … a fifth time … a sixth time. Time to give up? Never! A seventh prayer. A cloud! Followed by a downpour – **GOD ALWAYS KEEPS HIS PROMISES.**

You see, we have a part to play in bringing God's will about on earth. Even though God had promised rain, it was not until Elijah prayed – and kept praying – for rain that God opened the heavens to let it all pour out.

Don't get discouraged if you do not see immediate results from your prayers. God replies in the very best possible way – and always at the best time. What has God promised you? Claim those promises now.

ALL MAPPED OUT

'So I turned to the Lord God and pleaded with him in prayer and petition, in fasting, and in sackcloth and ashes. I prayed to the LORD my God and confessed: "Lord, the great and awesome God, who keeps his covenant of love with those who love him and keep his commandments, we have sinned and done wrong. We have been wicked and have rebelled; we have turned away from your commands and laws. We have not listened to your servants the prophets, who spoke in your name to our kings, our princes and our ancestors, and to all the people of the land."' **Daniel 9:3–6**

If God has the future all mapped out and has the power to do anything He wants, is there any point in praying? Daniel certainly thought so.

Daniel was an incredible ***OLD TESTAMENT HERO,*** a respected man of prayer. Well, what's going on in today's reading? Looks like we have caught him having his quiet time, and he is reading the book of Jeremiah. He was a teenager when the Jews were forced to work as slaves in Babylon, but now he is an old man.

Still, whatever age he was, ***HE APPRECIATED THE IMPORTANCE OF GOD'S WORD.***

As Daniel reads, he realises that God has put a limit on the time the Jews would be forced to live abroad – 70 years. He does a quick calculation … 'That's it, time's up!' So what does he do? He gets into serious talks with God to plead for the Jews to return to Jerusalem.

Daniel knew he had a part to play in God's plans. We, too, are God's partners, His agents and ambassadors here. Let's begin to grasp the fact that when we pray, we really are making a way for God to get involved in the situation. Don't you think that makes it incredibly exciting?

>ENGAGE

How about committing yourself now to pray regularly for a certain person or situation? Write the person's name or the situation on a piece of paper and put it in the front of your Bible or stick it on your wall, to remind you to pray.

UNDIVIDED

'Teach me your way, LORD, that I may rely on your faithfulness; give me an undivided heart, that I may fear your name. I will praise you, Lord my God, with all my heart; I will glorify your name for ever. For great is your love towards me; you have delivered me from the depths, from the realm of the dead.' **Psalm 86:11–13**

God wants us to talk to Him – ***HE WANTS US TO BE PART OF HIS PLANS.*** Our prayers open the way for Him to work. But prayer is more than that. It is building a relationship with God – to work with Him. But how?

If you want to get to know someone, what do you do? You chat to them! Because then you can begin to get to know more about them: things they are interested in, what they like, their opinions, hopes, etc.

Getting to know God is the same. It takes time to get to know Him. You need to spend time together, talking with Him, telling Him what's going on, seeing what He thinks about the things happening in your life.

David asked God for an undivided heart. What do you think that means? We have a divided heart when our love of other things, even other people, saps our love for God. Have you ever felt torn between having a quiet time with God and doing something else like watching a film? When we have a wholehearted love for God, **WE DON'T ALLOW ANYTHING TO PREVENT US FROM GETTING TO KNOW HIM BETTER.**

>ENGAGE

Are you struggling to find time each day to chat to God? Is prayer an optional extra to your daily schedule? How divided is your heart where God is concerned? It can all be put right by talking with Him now.

PRAY

Father, I want to spend time with You and I know You want to spend time with me. Thank You. Amen.

SPEND TIME

LOOK UP

'After Jesus said this, he looked towards heaven and prayed: "Father, the hour has come. Glorify your Son, that your Son may glorify you. For you granted him authority over all people that he might give eternal life to all those you have given him. Now this is eternal life: that they know you, the only true God, and Jesus Christ, whom you have sent. I have brought you glory on earth by finishing the work you gave me to do. And now, Father, glorify me in your presence with the glory I had with you before the world began."' **John 17:1–5**

Danger ahead! Look out! Or should it be 'look up'? When Jesus faced a terrifying ordeal, He knew who He had to look up to and what He should say.

Jesus was under great stress. He knew He was soon to be painfully crucified as a sacrifice for us. It was all in **GOD'S GREAT PLAN** to save the world. It was part of God's great purpose that Jesus would die (and be raised to life!). So Jesus prayed to His Father about the situation. He wanted to go through with God's plans so that others might have eternal life.

Prayer helps us to see situations from God's point of view. It puts us in a place where we can begin to understand and work with God. It's not pleading with God to fit into our plans but asking to get in line with His plans.

The issue of getting on with God can't be stressed enough! After all, this is the greatest part of Christianity – we can have a **MEANINGFUL RELATIONSHIP WITH GOD.** Get a load of this: Almighty God, the Creator of the universe, wants to get to know *you*.

>ENGAGE

Tell God what's on your mind. Tell Him about some of the things you have done recently or have got waiting for you. Tell Him that you want to know more about His plans for your life and go along with them.

KNOW YOU

ANY WHICH WAY

'Rejoice in the Lord always. I will say it again: Rejoice! Let your gentleness be evident to all. The Lord is near. Do not be anxious about anything, but in every situation, by prayer and petition, with thanksgiving, present your requests to God. And the peace of God, which transcends all understanding, will guard your hearts and your minds in Christ Jesus.' **Philippians 4:4–7**

So far we have established the main reasons why we pray. Now let's get down to the practicality of *how* we pray.

HOW DOES GOD WANT ME TO PRAY? Is there a particular set of words to use? Should I stand up or kneel down? Well, posture, place, time and language seem to be of little importance to God. Why? Just look at the prayers in the Bible: They prayed ...

- sitting (2 Sam. 7:18)
- lying face down (Matt. 26:39)
- with hands lifted up (Psa. 28:2)
- silently (1 Sam. 1:13)
- aloud (Ezek. 11:13)
- alone (Mark 1:35)

- together (Acts 4:24)
- at fixed times (Psa. 55:17)
- anytime (Luke 18:1)
- in bed (Psa. 63:6)
- in fields (Gen. 24:11–12)
- in the Temple (2 Kings 19:14–15)
- at the riverside (Acts 16:13)
- on the seashore (Acts 21:5)
- even on the battlefield (1 Sam. 7:5).

>ENGAGE

In the Bible, people didn't seem to mind when or where they talked to God. And neither should we! God is really interested in the attitude of our hearts. Why not arrange to meet up with other young people from your church to pray together, or just pray now?

KNOW HOW

JUST ASK

'I write these things to you who believe in the name of the Son of God so that you may know that you have eternal life. This is the confidence we have in approaching God: that if we ask anything according to his will, he hears us. And if we know that he hears us – whatever we ask – we know that we have what we asked of him.' **1 John 5:13–15**

Prayer sounds pretty laid back, doesn't it? Saying what you want, how you want it and when you want it. Well, not quite … Over the next few days we'll look at some of the conditions for a successful prayer life.

To have a successful prayer life, do we need to stop watching TV, shave our heads and sit in a pile of ashes? No, but we do need to **LEARN TO PRAY IN GOD'S WILL.**

But how do we know what God wants? Ask Him! If you wanted to know what your best friend wanted or was thinking about, you'd ask and **LISTEN TO THE REPLY.**

We also have the Bible to guide us. We may not get specific answers to our questions (eg, who should I go out with?) but we can learn God's guidelines for living (eg, the sort of people we should or shouldn't form deep relationships with). So, by knowing what the Bible says and talking to God about the situations that we face, we can work out what He wants us to do.

Verse 15 tells us that if we ask anything according to His will, we know that He hears us. Brilliant! We also need a good measure of the 'fear' of the Lord (which means an awesome respect) when we talk to Him. This causes us to listen to God before listening to anyone else.

Why not take some time to ask God if there is anything on His heart that He would like to talk to you about? Keep thinking about God and who He is – He will talk to you.

ASK

THE BIG IMPRESSION

ARE YOU LISTENING?

'Then a great and powerful wind tore the mountains apart and shattered the rocks before the LORD, but the LORD was not in the wind. After the wind there was an earthquake, but the LORD was not in the earthquake. After the earthquake came a fire, but the LORD was not in the fire. And after the fire came a gentle whisper. When Elijah heard it, he pulled his cloak over his face and went out and stood at the mouth of the cave.' **1 Kings 19:11–13**

God gave us all two ears and one mouth – is that because we need to listen twice as much as we speak? Well, as far as prayer is concerned, ***WE NEED TO LISTEN FAR MORE THAN WE DO.***

Here's Elijah, a few days after seeing God work miracles – but is he celebrating? No, he is in a deep, dark, depressed mood, wanting to end it all.

So how did God let Elijah know that He was around and loved him dearly? Did He quickly breeze past or shake him up or fire him? No, God spoke quietly to reassure Elijah. And the gloomy prophet listened, knew it was God speaking and got ***BACK INTO ACTION.***

How do we know when we are hearing God's voice? Well, it's not usually an outer or audible voice. This is not to say that it never happens: people have heard God in that way. More usually though, it's like an inner impression that can be difficult to pin down sometimes. A bit like the way you talk to yourself without anyone being able to hear. God sometimes speaks to us in a quiet inner way.

>ENGAGE

What has God said to you through the Bible today? Ask Him if there is anything more He would like to tell you.

PRAY

Father, help me to hear Your voice – now as I sit here and later as I go about my day. Amen.

LISTEN

'I warn everyone who hears the words of the prophecy of this scroll: if anyone adds anything to them, God will add to that person the plagues described in this scroll. And if anyone takes words away from this scroll of prophecy, God will take away from that person any share in the tree of life and in the Holy City, which are described in this scroll.'

Revelation 22:18–19

So, God sometimes speaks to us in a quiet inner way. But how do we know it's God speaking to us, and not just our own thoughts?

One thing to remember is that God never says one thing one minute and the opposite thing the next. **HE NEVER CONTRADICTS ANYTHING HE HAS WRITTEN IN THE BIBLE.** So, if you think God is telling you to do something that goes against what the Bible says, you're mistaken.

Also remember that **GOD'S QUIET INNER VOICE DOES NOT ARGUE, IS NEVER PUSHY AND WILL NEVER TEASE OR TRICK YOU.** The Holy Spirit is not brash but gently impresses Himself on your spirit.

When you talk to a close friend on the phone, you immediately recognise their voice. You hear them so often their voice is familiar. But if someone you've not heard from for ages calls out of the blue, you may not recognise their voice at first. It's the same with our ability to hear and recognise God's voice.

The more time we spend listening to God speaking to us through the Bible and that 'inner voice' in our hearts, the more easily we will recognise when it really is Him speaking to us.

Get a notebook, pen and Bible. Find a quiet place. Ask God to remind you of a passage we have looked at. Read it again. Write down what you think God is saying.

RECOGNISE

GLAD YOU ASKED

'"Because he loves me," says the LORD, "I will rescue him; I will protect him, for he acknowledges my name. He will call on me, and I will answer him; I will be with him in trouble, I will deliver him and honour him. With long life I will satisfy him and show him my salvation."'

Psalm 91:14–16

Should we go to God with a shopping list of things we want Him to do for us? Place your order with God and await delivery. Sounds easy, doesn't it? So what's in the small print? Why do we sometimes think God has not answered our prayers? Well, God doesn't dispatch goodies from heaven just because we want them. **THERE ARE TERMS AND CONDITIONS FOR ANSWERED PRAYER** and we'll look at some of these over the next few days.

Before we do this, it's important to realise that it's always OK to ask God for things. Ever heard someone say, 'But what if I'm asking for something I shouldn't?' or 'I'm not sure if it's God's will or not'? Well, what about when we ask our earthly parents for things?

If we've got it wrong they won't mind – they'll be glad we asked – and they only want what is best for us. How much more will our heavenly Father give what is best for us, and only deny things that may harm us (Matt. 7:9–11). That's why the Bible says, 'If any of you lacks wisdom, you should ask God, who gives generously to all without finding fault, and it will be given to you' (James 1:5).

>ENGAGE

God doesn't expect us to be all-knowing, wise and wonderful. He wants us to be honest with Him and trust that He knows best. So why not talk to Him right now?

PRAY

Thank You, Lord, that when we ask, You come alongside us and show us how and what to pray. Please help me to pray right now … in the name of Jesus. Amen.

'I cried out to him with my mouth; his praise was on my tongue. If I had cherished sin in my heart, the Lord would not have listened; but God has surely listened and has heard my prayer. Praise be to God, who has not rejected my prayer or withheld his love from me!'

Psalm 66:17–20

So why don't some prayers get answered? Let's take a look at some of the reasons why God doesn't seem to spring into action as soon as we ask Him.

We might be holding onto something that we don't want God to deal with

It may be that we want the best of both worlds. We want God's blessings but we also want to enjoy things we know would displease God. That doesn't work. It could be that, before God will act, He needs to hear a heartfelt 'sorry' from us first. Our relationship with Him needs to be **RESTORED** so that we can sort out our priorities and work things out together. **HE IS ALWAYS WILLING TO FORGIVE US,** dust us off and put us back on our feet again.

We might be praying in a selfish way

We might be praying with only our personal interests in mind – and not God's glory! You know, those 'please give me …' prayers. We spend our time telling God what we want rather than asking Him what we need in order to live for Him. Check out your heart and see if your prayers revolve around you or God.

Have a think about the sort of prayers you've been praying lately. Could you change the way you pray at all? Pray for God's will to be done in your life today and see what happens …!

NO GRUDGES

'"And forgive us our debts, as we also have forgiven our debtors ..." For if you forgive other people when they sin against you, your heavenly Father will also forgive you. But if you do not forgive others their sins, your Father will not forgive your sins.'

Matthew 6:12,14–15

We'll carry on with one more reason why prayers might sometimes not be answered (or not answered right away or in the way we want, that is). This is such a brilliant and challenging piece of scripture from the Bible that it could really do with a whole book all to itself – and it's all about forgiveness.

We might need to forgive someone first

Holding a grudge against someone is **ONE OF THE BIGGEST HINDRANCES TO PRAYER** and one of the most destructive things a person can do to himself. **UNFORGIVENESS IS LIKE A DISEASE.** It spreads and begins to affect the whole body, and if it's not treated it will poison the soul. Is there someone you need to forgive?

God tells us the same thing in Mark 11:25–26 (verse 26 is a footnote in the NIV). He won't answer until you repent of any unforgiveness. It's serious business!

>ENGAGE

If God is speaking to you about this, or if you are eaten up with bitterness, God can set you free. Talk with Him about it or find someone you trust and pray together about the matter. As you pray, ask the Holy Spirit to come and make you pure once again. Then enjoy the freedom that He brings.

PRAY

Father, even though I might not feel like it, I forgive (person's name) and ask You to bless them. Thank You that You forgave me. Amen.

FORGIVE

ATTACHED

'I am the vine; you are the branches. If you remain in me and I in you, you will bear much fruit; apart from me you can do nothing. If you do not remain in me, you are like a branch that is thrown away and withers; such branches are picked up, thrown into the fire and burned. If you remain in me and my words remain in you, ask whatever you wish, and it will be done for you. This is to my Father's glory, that you bear much fruit, showing yourselves to be my disciples.' **John 15:5–8**

Jesus is speaking the words in today's reading. But what is He talking about? Let's think about ourselves as branches (just go with it!) ...

Detached from the vine

A wild, unruly branch with lots of dead wood and little fruit. A picture of those who are not living close to God. They do not allow God to deal with the wrong things in their lives and they shut the Holy Spirit out.

Attached to the vine

A tidy branch laden with clusters of grapes. Christians who have a **CLOSE RELATIONSHIP** with God allow Him to deal with disobedience in their lives so the fruit of the Holy Spirit (love, joy, peace, patience etc) can grow.

So, the promise is that as we obey Jesus and walk closely with Him, we will know what to pray, and whatever we ask we will receive from Him. Wow! But prayer is not an occasional nod in God's direction. We need to keep at it. **BE PERSISTENT! BE BOLD!** If we know God is behind us, let's be determined to keep praying until the job gets done. That could be days, weeks, even years. But hang on in there and see God do some amazing things with your life, friends and family.

Do you want to be closer to God today? Remember, He is faithful and He keeps all His promises. Talk with Him now.

BEHIND THEIR BACKS

'And this is my prayer: that your love may abound more and more in knowledge and depth of insight, so that you may be able to discern what is best and may be pure and blameless for the day of Christ, filled with the fruit of righteousness that comes through Jesus Christ – to the glory and praise of God.' **Philippians 1:9–11**

Prayer is a wonderful opportunity to talk about other people behind their backs. But not in the way you might think! It's not to gossip about them but to talk to God about their needs.

When Paul visited Philippi on his second missionary journey, several people became Christians. Lydia (a successful businesswoman) and a prison jailer were among those who came to Christ and formed the ***FIRST CHRISTIAN CHURCH IN EUROPE.*** Paul wrote to them to tell them that he was praying for them. Just look at his love and prayers for them:

- I'm so grateful for all your help in telling others about Jesus …
- God continues to do ***GOOD THINGS*** in your lives …

- You are very special …
- I pray you will overflow with love for others … and witness by your kindness.
- Learn more from the Bible and understand it.

What a great prayer! Who could you be praying for today? When you meet with a group of Christians, why not discuss how you could pray for each other? Maybe you could regularly meet with one or two other friends. Not only could you pray for one another but you could pray for some of your friends and family, who don't know Jesus, too.

PRAY

THE KEYS TO THE KINGDOM

'I will give you the keys of the kingdom of heaven; whatever you bind on earth will be bound in heaven, and whatever you loose on earth will be loosed in heaven.'

Matthew 16:19

As we come to the end of our study on prayer, the big question is – are you on better talking terms with God? Prayer is not something to study but to practise. It's the key to our relationship with God.

Remember some of the key things we have learnt about prayer …

- We were **CREATED TO COMMUNICATE WITH GOD** but sin brought down the connection. Through Jesus we're reconnected so we can talk to God.
- Prayer is our personal link to God to express ourselves to Him about anything at any time.
- **THE HOLY SPIRIT HELPS US TO PRAY.**
- Our prayers have a part to play in making God's plans happen.
- Prayer is not pleading with God to fit into our plans but asking to get in line with His.

- We must have an awesome respect for God when we talk to Him.
- Sin, selfishness and unforgiveness are hindrances to our relationship with God.
- We should pray for others.
- God wants us to talk to Him.

>ENGAGE

God has given us the keys to open any situation to His power. The question is whether we leave the keys in our pocket, or start turning the lock.

PRAY

Jesus, thank You that You want to come into all areas of my life. Teach me how to pray so that Your power is unlocked in my life and in the situations I face. Teach me how to love and pray for others too. Amen.

FROM ZERO TO HERO

'When they arrived, Samuel saw Eliab and thought, "Surely the LORD's anointed stands here before the LORD." But the LORD said to Samuel, "Do not consider his appearance or his height, for I have rejected him. The LORD does not look at the things people look at. People look at the outward appearance, but the LORD looks at the heart."' **1 Samuel 16:6–7**

Let's dive into the story of singer-songwriter David – the harpist who made it to the top the hard way. Despite a **GIANT HIT** early on, he had to wait several years before his big break. God still had a few things he needed to teach David – all of them relevant to us today.

David was the youngest of eight brothers – the last in the pecking order. He was probably bossed around and picked on by his older brothers. His prospects of being anything but a humble shepherd were zero. And when God sent Samuel to choose one of the brothers as the next king of Israel, David was not even called for an audition.

Samuel thought David's eldest brother, Eliab, was a dead cert for the job. He had everything going for him.

But **GOD DOES NOT JUDGE PEOPLE BY THEIR APPEARANCE.** He knows how they think and behave. And in this area, all of David's older brothers were lacking the qualities God wanted. Eventually David was called for interview and God gave him the job, as well as the power of the Holy Spirit to do it well.

Do you ever feel insignificant or down because others seem to have more going for them than you do? Well, you don't need to feel like that. Why? Because God knows you are important. He has actually chosen you to be in His family (Eph. 1:4). Think about the ways God shows that He values you – and praise Him for each one.

CHOSEN

A GIANT PROBLEM

'Now the Israelites had been saying, "Do you see how this man keeps coming out? He comes out to defy Israel. The king will give great wealth to the man who kills him. He will also give him his daughter in marriage and will exempt his family from taxes in Israel." David asked the men standing near him, "What will be done for the man who kills this Philistine and removes this disgrace from Israel? Who is this uncircumcised Philistine that he should defy the armies of the living God?"'

1 Samuel 17:25–26

Ever faced a giant problem? Not just a bit of hassle, but a difficult situation of King Kong proportions. How did you cope? When Goliath appeared on the scene, David and his older brothers had a choice – flight or fight.

We begin to see why God chose David as king and not his eldest brother Eliab. When faced with nine feet of muscle and brawn in the shape of Goliath, Eliab ran away (along with the rest of the Israelite army). David, on a visit to the camp, knew he couldn't overcome the overgrown Philistine hulk – but God could.

Eliab's other weakness came to the surface when he was under pressure. When he heard David talking tough, pointing out the disgrace of running away and failing to trust God, he was angry and jealous. His baby brother should be at home looking after the sheep, not showing him up. Eliab accused David of being big-headed and wicked. But **DAVID WAS NOT BOASTING ABOUT HIS OWN POWER BUT GOD'S.** He was prepared to face the giant problem in God's strength.

Eliab's remarks did not deter David. Don't be put off if people try to belittle your faith in God.

>ENGAGE

God says we don't need to run away or hide from any large problem in our lives. He wants us to sling the matter over to Him because He has the power to deal with it. Don't keep churning a problem over in your mind. Talk with God about anything that worries you and ask Him to show you the best way to overcome your problems or fears.

ONE STEP AT A TIME

'"All those gathered here will know that it is not by sword or spear that the LORD saves; for the battle is the LORD's, and he will give all of you into our hands." As the Philistine moved closer to attack him, David ran quickly towards the battle line to meet him. Reaching into his bag and taking out a stone, he slung it and struck the Philistine on the forehead. The stone sank into his forehead, and he fell face down on the ground. So David triumphed over the Philistine with a sling and a stone; without a sword in his hand he struck down the Philistine and killed him.' **1 Samuel 17:47–50**

It was one of the most uneven contests of all time. Goliath was the undefeated super-heavyweight champion of the world. **DAVID HAD FOUGHT A LION AND A BEAR,** but no one gave the musical shepherd a chance in this title fight.

In the red corner, all the way from Gath ... the super heavyweight champion of the world – Goliath. In the blue corner, from Bethlehem in Judea ... the unknown featherweight shepherd – David. Ding ding. Round one.

Goliath stomps out of his corner and leads with a jab to David's ear (a curse from one of his gods). He follows it up with a left-right combination about David being made into bird fodder. David takes it on the chin and leads with a jab that God will cut Goliath down to size. Another jab from David, claiming the championship is the Lord's ... Goliath lumbers towards David. The youngster slings a shot to Goliath's head. The champion is out for the count!

David didn't worry about the situation. He trusted God and went forward a step at a time. If you are faced with a giant-sized problem, try not to worry how you are going to deal with it. If you are part of God's family you have a heavenly Father to help you sort it out. You are not alone in the struggle, so talk with God about anything that worries you.

Father, help me to trust You, whatever the size of my problems. Give me confidence through knowing You are with me. Amen.

LOYAL TO THE END

'And Jonathan made a covenant with David because he loved him as himself.'

1 Samuel 18:3

King Saul's son, Jonathan, the heir to the throne, became David's closest friend. Is this surprising? It is when **GOD HAS CHOSEN DAVID** to be king instead of Jonathan.

Following the giant clash, David was invited to stay at the palace. And another giant clash was expected. How would David and Jonathan hit it off – literally? They were both in line to be the next king of Israel. Jonathan was the rightful heir to the throne. However, because his father, King Saul, had been disobedient, God intended to take the throne from Saul's family. David had already been anointed as Saul's successor. Would the two lads become bitter rivals?

Remarkably, **THEY GOT ON WELL AND BECAME CLOSE FRIENDS** – so much so that they made a solemn promise to remain loyal to each other for the rest of their lives. Jonathan was prepared to let God have His way and generously gave David the status symbols of a prince.

David: the early years

Favourite clothes: I used to wear a shepherd's tunic, but when I made the big time I was kitted out by Jonathan with a designer-label royal robe and ornamental belt from the fashion houses of Babylon.

Most treasured possession: My heavy metal outfit. There were only two metal swords in Israel and they belonged to Saul and Jonathan. Jonathan honoured me by giving me his highly prized iron sword.

Best friend: Jonathan is and always will be my best friend. We have promised to remain friends no matter what the future holds for us.

Some friends are like your shadow – you only see them when the sun shines, meaning they're only around when life is fun and easy. What is your attitude to your friends? If we use our friends we will lose our friends. True friendship is developed when we give to others the consideration we give to ourselves. Why not spend time praying for your friends?

SPEAR OF JEALOUSY

'Saul was afraid of David, because the LORD was with David but had departed from Saul. So he sent David away from him and gave him command over a thousand men, and David led the troops in their campaigns. In everything he did he had great success, because the LORD was with him.' **1 Samuel 18:12–14**

Jonathan may have been prepared to accept David as the next king of Israel, but Saul had other ideas.

Saul was swamped by hundreds of women as he returned from battle – and loved every minute of it, until he realised that most were members of David's newly formed fan club.

The catchy tambourine jingle they sang got on his nerves. It implied that David had done ten times better than he had. And to make matters worse, the song developed into a nationwide hit.

David's **BRAVE EXPLOITS IN BATTLE** had made him everyone's pin-up hero. Jealous Saul decided to pin David up on his wall – with a spear.

It was the first of several attempts Saul was to make on David's life. David had to rely on God to protect him from Saul and the Philistines. And **GOD NEVER LET HIM DOWN.** He gave the young army commander success in all he did and the song remained at number one – to Saul's annoyance.

>ENGAGE

Following God's plan for our lives isn't always easy, but we can always know that God is with us. Pray with a friend or family member that God will protect you from danger and help you remember that He is always with you, just as He was with David.

PRAY

Lord, thank You for always being with me and for helping me in life's battle. Amen.

BAND OF WARRIORS

'David left Gath and escaped to the cave of Adullam. When his brothers and his father's household heard about it, they went down to him there. All those who were in distress or in debt or discontented gathered round him, and he became their commander. About four hundred men were with him.'

1 Samuel 22:1–2

From palace harpist and Israel's favourite bloke, to a fugitive hiding in caves from Saul and his men. But David did not remain alone for long. His family knew their lives would be threatened and came to join him. About 400 men, many with grudges against Saul, some of them criminals, joined David's band of warriors. This was ***NO ROMANTIC ROBIN HOOD EXISTENCE*** with succulent venison dinners. The land was wild and rocky, dry and dusty, full of hidden dangers. Food and water were scarce.

However, despite his problems, David was concerned for his parents' welfare and went to great lengths to see that they received proper care. It was also a great test of David's leadership qualities, and he emerged as the ***NATURAL LEADER*** of the travelling band.

Each man had arrived with a history of discontentment, fear and failure. David was able to help them put the past behind them and work together to carry out **GOD'S PLANS FOR THEIR LIVES.**

>ENGAGE

It must have been really hard for David when he became a fugitive. He told the king of Moab that he needed time to learn what God was going to do for him. When our lives are turned upside down by sudden changes in circumstances, we need to let God teach us new things through our experiences. And even in the most miserable circumstances, we should try to care for those around us. Ask God to teach you new things about Him today.

TEACH US

THE PEACEKEEPER

'Praise be to the LORD, the God of Israel, who has sent you today to meet me. May you be blessed for your good judgment and for keeping me from bloodshed this day and from avenging myself with my own hands.' **1 Samuel 25:32 –33**

David had treated Nabal's men and cattle well. But when Nabal refused to return the favour, David's **BLOOD BOILED** with rage. He really blew his stack. Nobody treats a harpist like that and gets away with it!

It can be really annoying when you do something good for someone who doesn't repay your kindness or even acknowledge you or say 'thanks'.

But anger isn't the right response. It's not helpful for you or the person you're angry with. Anger spells danger (just add a 'd'!). In a fit of rage, David wanted revenge at any cost. 'David – never heard of him,' Nabal had said. 'I'll show him who David is,' was the response ... or might aswell have been.

If God had not sent Nabal's wife, Abigail, to intervene, a bloody battle would have resulted – all over some food. Abigail's arrival with a takeaway meal brought David to his senses. He realised what a fool he had been and how close he had come to murder.

>ENGAGE

You are never a dynamic person because you blow your top. And hot words never lead to cool decisions. God wants you to have a warm heart not a hot head. So, if you tend to get wound up about things and lose your temper, step back, take a minute and spend some time talking it over with God.

PRAY

Father, help me to keep calm and to talk to You about what is going on when I get wound up. Show me how I should respond, what I should say and what I should do. Amen.

KEEP CALM

LET HIM DEAL WITH IT

'When David heard that Nabal was dead, he said, "Praise be to the LORD, who has upheld my cause against Nabal for treating me with contempt. He has kept his servant from doing wrong and has brought Nabal's wrongdoing down on his own head."' **1 Samuel 25:39**

When we are treated unfairly, it's tempting to get hot under the collar and take the matter into our own hands. But is that the best way? David learnt that ***IT IS BETTER TO LET GOD SORT THINGS OUT.*** And just look how God dealt with Nabal.

Nabal was a wicked man. He was a fool by name (v25) and a fool by nature. The drunken farmer had no idea that his wife, Abigail, had saved his life by getting a takeaway meal to David. He was too busy whooping it up at a wild party. In the morning, as he sobered up, his wife explained what she had done. It was all too much for Nabal – he had a heart attack and died ten days later.

David was thankful he had not gone ahead and taken the law into his own hands. God had stopped him and dealt with Nabal instead. Often when we are dealt with unfairly we want to see justice done immediately.

And if we see that someone appears to be getting away with it, we can get pretty uptight. God wants us to **LET HIM DEAL WITH THESE SITUATIONS.** He knows about the injustices in our world and the villains await His judgment. No one messes with God and escapes the consequences of their actions.

>ENGAGE

Incidents that make us angry can continue to wind us up as we look back on them. It is important that we take these matters to God and leave Him to deal with them in His way and His time. After all, no one enjoys being bitter.

PRAY

Lord, help me to talk things over with You before deciding what to do next, and to deal with any bitterness I feel towards those who have upset me in the past. Amen.

REVENGE IS ... BITTER

'But David said to Abishai, "Don't destroy him! Who can lay a hand on the LORD's anointed and be guiltless? As surely as the LORD lives," he said, "the LORD himself will strike him, or his time will come and he will die, or he will go into battle and perish. But the LORD forbid that I should lay a hand on the LORD's anointed. Now get the spear and water jug that are near his head, and let's go."' **1 Samuel 26:9–11**

Had David learnt not to act on impulse? Was he now prepared to wait and let God sort things out? The big test came soon after the incident with Nabal, when he had a golden opportunity to assassinate Saul and become king.

Twice Saul had tried to pin David to the wall with a spear. Now David has the opportunity to pin Saul to the ground with the same weapon. In one plunge he could get rid of the man who was hunting him down and become king of Israel. After all, God had told David he would become king, hadn't He?

David's row with Nabal had taught him not to act rashly. Yes, God wanted David to be king of Israel, but not by murdering Saul. To kill Saul would be **COMPLETELY OUT OF ORDER.**

No, David must wait patiently for God to deal with Saul and give him the crown. He had to let God do it His way. David took Saul's highly prized metal spear to let the king know he had spared his life. But he didn't want to be guilty of theft either. He left the spear for one of Saul's men to recover (v22).

We should never go about doing something that is right in the wrong way. Not only do our motives need to be right but **OUR ACTIONS SHOULD BE RIGHT TOO.** David realised that when he started to do things his way, there was every chance things could go seriously wrong. It is always best to talk to God about everything you do and let Him bring about His plans for you in the right way and at the right time.

Look up and learn Psalm 37:7–9. Ask the Lord to help you 'wait patiently' for Him.

ACTIONS

RESCUE MISSION

'When David and his men reached Ziklag, they found it destroyed by fire and their wives and sons and daughters taken captive. So David and his men wept aloud until they had no strength left to weep. David's two wives had been captured – Ahinoam of Jezreel and Abigail, the widow of Nabal of Carmel. David was greatly distressed because the men were talking of stoning him; each one was bitter in spirit because of his sons and daughters. David found strength in the LORD his God.'

1 Samuel 30:3–6

David's songs were usually lively, cheerful numbers. But the events at Ziklag were to leave him singing the blues.

David and his men were ***ABSOLUTELY GUTTED.*** While they had been away, the Amalekites had raided their base at Ziklag and kidnapped their wives and children. The men wept till they dropped to the ground in grief.

David was distraught. And to make matters worse, his men were turning their anger and bitterness on him. There was even talk of killing him.

What was David to do? Wisely, **HE TOOK THE MATTER TO GOD,** who promised him success if he stormed after the hijackers. David set off with his best men and gate-crashed the Amalekite party. The hijackers were put out of action and all the hostages were released. It was a highly successful rescue mission – thanks to God.

>ENGAGE

Some events in life can be so devastating that even the toughest of people find it difficult to cope. David knew he did not have the strength to deal with the situation and wisely turned to God for advice and help. Trusting the Lord in times of trouble is never easy, but as we do, He can use our faith to encourage others as well as us.

PRAY

Father, help me to stick close to You through thick and thin, in good times and in bad. Amen.

WORTH THE WAIT

'"And the LORD said to you, 'You shall shepherd my people Israel, and you shall become their ruler.'" When all the elders of Israel had come to King David at Hebron, the king made a covenant with them at Hebron before the LORD, and they anointed David king over Israel. David was thirty years old when he became king, and he reigned for forty years. In Hebron he reigned over Judah for seven years and six months, and in Jerusalem he reigned over all Israel and Judah for thirty-three years.'

2 Samuel 5:2–5

Saul is killed in battle and David is crowned king. It should be a time of celebration for David, but he still sings the blues.

Saul and Jonathan had both died defending Israel against the Philistines (1 Sam. 31). The remarkable thing is that David not only mourned over Jonathan's death but over the death of his arch enemy, Saul. Although Saul had become a spiritual disaster zone, David still recognised he had been **GOD'S ANOINTED LEADER** and was saddened at Saul's collapse.

At first, David was anointed king over Judah in the south, but soon the whole nation recognised him as their king. The boy-shepherd was now God's 'shepherd', caring for the nation of Israel.

David knew he was going to become king but it was many years before God's promises came true. And David didn't try to make it happen himself but **WAITED FOR GOD TO BRING IT ABOUT.** Waiting is tough – especially when we have asked God for something we feel sure is right. God uses the waiting period to prepare us for the things that lie ahead. And the great thing about God is that the wait is always worth it.

If you feel frustrated that God appears to be delaying certain things in your life, read 2 Peter 3:8–9. Ask God for the patience to wait for Him to answer in the best possible way.

WAIT

LOOKS CAN BE DECEIVING

'David then took up residence in the fortress and called it the City of David. He built up the area around it, from the terraces inwards. And he became more and more powerful, because the LORD God Almighty was with him. Now Hiram king of Tyre sent envoys to David, along with cedar logs and carpenters and stonemasons, and they built a palace for David. Then David knew that the LORD had established him as king over Israel and had exalted his kingdom for the sake of his people Israel.' **2 Samuel 5:9–12**

David lived in Hebron when he became king, but he needed a more central and defensible capital city. His attention turned to a place called Jebus (which many historians believe is what we now know as Jerusalem), which was occupied by the Jebusites. But the city appeared ***IMPOSSIBLE TO CAPTURE.***

The Jebusites were so confident that no one could break through the sturdy battlements of their city that they mocked David and his men.

But they had underestimated David. He led his men up the secret water tunnel the Jebusites used to bring water to the city when it was under siege. David caught the enemy by surprise and secured the city as the capital of the Israelites. Jerusalem is still known as the City of David today.

In verse 10, David shares the secret of his success – he became more and more powerful because **THE LORD WAS WITH HIM.**

>ENGAGE

If we want the Lord to be with us, we must want to be with the Lord. Have a chat with your Christian friends and ask them what they find tough about being a Christian. Share your thoughts about it as well. You could tell them some of the things you have learnt from your study of David so far. Why not pray with them and ask God to help you to stay close to Him?

PRAY

Father, please help me and my friends to stay close to You and live Your way. Amen.

AMBITIONS

'After the king was settled in his palace and the LORD had given him rest from all his enemies around him, he said to Nathan the prophet, "Here I am, living in a house of cedar, while the ark of God remains in a tent." Nathan replied to the king, "Whatever you have in mind, go ahead and do it, for the LORD is with you."'

2 Samuel 7:1–3

David imported sweet-smelling cedar wood to build his dream palace. As he relaxed in his en suite jacuzzi, he had a twinge of conscience. Here he was living in luxury while the ark of the covenant (which symbolised God being with His people) was kept in a tent. David had what seemed like such a good idea ... and the prophet Nathan was so sure that God would rubber-stamp the project, he gave the go-ahead without asking Him.

God did want a temple, but He did not want David to build it. In **GOD'S PROJECT-PLANNING,** the Temple was scheduled to be built by David's successor. The news came as a shock to Nathan and David.

How did David react when God put his idea on hold? Would David go ahead regardless or try to bring the schedule forward?

David rejoiced in **THE GOOD THINGS GOD PROMISED TO DO IN THE FUTURE.** He was excited that God was going to keep the throne in his family and that the Temple would be built – even if he would not be alive to see it.

David reacted positively to this set-back to his plans. He bought a plot of land for the Temple and gathered quality building materials ready for his son to take on the project.

>ENGAGE

It is never easy to give up our plans, dreams or ambitions when the Lord shows He has other plans for us. Neither is it easy to hand over a project that was your idea to someone else (and see them get the credit). The lesson to be learnt is that we need to share all our ideas and plans with God. If we go ahead without consulting Him, we risk bringing confusion to the situation. Why not share some of your plans, ambitions and ideas with God now?

A MAN OF HIS WORD

'When Mephibosheth son of Jonathan, the son of Saul, came to David, he bowed down to pay him honour.
David said, "Mephibosheth!"
"At your service," he replied.
"Don't be afraid," David said to him, "for I will surely show you kindness for the sake of your father Jonathan. I will restore to you all the land that belonged to your grandfather Saul, and you will always eat at my table."
Mephibosheth bowed down and said, "What is your servant, that you should notice a dead dog like me?"'

2 Samuel 9:6–8

It was the custom for a new king to wipe out the remaining relatives of the last monarch and anyone else with a claim to the throne. Saul had one remaining relative, Jonathan's son, a man called Mephibosheth, who had a disability in both feet. Would David order his execution?

Mephibosheth had broken his legs as a youngster and they had not healed properly. He became a disabled fugitive with low self-esteem – describing himself as a 'dead dog' (v8). As he hobbled into the palace,

HE WAS EXPECTING THE WORST BUT HE GOT THE BEST. Not only did David spare his life but he was treated as a prince. He was given land, servants and the honour of eating at the king's table.

Why did David show such kindness to a potential enemy? David had promised Jonathan that he would always treat his family well. And David kept his promise.

>ENGAGE

This is a brilliant picture of what God has done for us. Even though we have turned away from God, He doesn't give us the treatment we deserve. Instead, He loves us, forgives us and welcomes us into His family. Do you sometimes come to God expecting the worst? God loves you. He promises to look after you. He keeps His promises. When we come to God we can expect the best. Never shy away from God because you feel like a 'dead dog' Christian. Go on and talk with Him and be ready for His welcome.

DECEPTION

'One evening David got up from his bed and walked around on the roof of the palace. From the roof he saw a woman washing. The woman was very beautiful, and David sent someone to find out about her. The man said, "She is Bathsheba, the daughter of Eliam and the wife of Uriah the Hittite." Then David sent messengers to get her.'

2 Samuel 11:2–4

David was experienced in handling the affairs of state. But there was one affair that left him *in* a state.

David knew it was totally **OUT OF ORDER** to have an affair with another man's wife. But after eyeing up Bathsheba from a distance, he got carried away. One thing led to another and …

The casual one-night stand was disastrous. Bathsheba became pregnant. The affair could not be concealed. David was prepared to go to any length to prevent a royal scandal. While David was prepared to break every rule in the book to conceal his guilt, in contrast, Bathsheba's husband, Uriah, was **A MAN OF HONOUR.**

David schemed to fool Uriah into thinking he was the father of the baby. But Uriah was not prepared to spend a comfortable night with his wife while his fellow troops were living rough on the battlefield.

David was stumped! He could see it in the tabloids – front-page headline! Would the scandal bring down his government? He hatched another desperate cover-up plan.

>ENGAGE

It is easy to let our desire for sexual pleasure run riot. We become especially vulnerable if we are continually eyeing up the other sex improperly. That's why we would be wise to avoid adult films, dodgy websites and stuff like that. David thought he was man enough to handle it but it really messed up his life. Ask God to keep your passions under His control. Yes, you have a heavenly Father who you can talk to freely and frankly about these matters. Try it!

BE WISE

AT WHAT COST?

'When Uriah's wife heard that her husband was dead, she mourned for him. After the time of mourning was over, David had her brought to his house, and she became his wife and bore him a son. But the thing David had done displeased the LORD.' **2 Samuel 11:26–27**

A scandal is about to break out unless David acts quickly. This story must be silenced at all costs. The harpist is right out of tune with God.

David was in a **DOWNWARD SPIRAL OF LIES** and now he's hit an all-time low. Once again he has the chance to admit what he's done, to come clean, but instead of acknowledging what he has done and 'fessing up, he covers up and the result is serious. So serious it costs a man his life.

King David ordered General Joab to put Uriah out on the front line, to attack the most heavily defended part of the city wall, and it was a suicide mission. It was almost definitely intended by David to be the end of Uriah – and it was.

And after all this, David finally gets what he wants. **BUT AT WHAT COST?** This talented musician and 'man after [God's] own heart' (Acts 13:22) has allowed his sin and guilt to come between himself and God.

Separated, he can't seem to write any more psalms in worship. Is there any hope for our fallen hero?

>ENGAGE

When we cover our tracks to conceal wrong, we may think we've gotten away with it. That's never true: everything we do affects others in some way, good or bad. Worst of all, breaking God's rules separates us from Him. David stopped writing psalms at this time because his close relationship with God was broken. Don't try to conceal anything from God. Be open with Him.

PRAY

Father, I'm sorry for when I mess up. I don't want to be separated from You. Please always show me how I can make things right again, with Your help. Amen.

CONSE-QUENCES

'Then David said to Nathan, "I have sinned against the LORD." Nathan replied, "The LORD has taken away your sin. You are not going to die. But because by doing this you have shown utter contempt for the LORD, the son born to you will die."'

2 Samuel 12:13–14

The tabloids have it. Scandal at the palace! God has leaked the story.

Nathan didn't confront David with the sordid truth, but told him a parable that was a mirror image of David's wrongdoing (which you can read in 2 Samuel 12). When David heard how a rich man had made mincemeat of a poor man's much loved lamb, he was incensed! 'This rich man deserves to die!' David announced, not realising that he was judging himself.

When David got clued up to the fact he had acted like the rich man in stealing Uriah's wife, he fell apart with regret. He **OWNED UP** to his wickedness and faced the sad consequences of his actions.

Shocking news: **King admits to secret love affair**
King David was in hiding today after **DRAMATIC REVELATIONS** that he arranged for Uriah to be killed to conceal a secret affair with Bathsheba.

The king is said to be deeply sorry for the distress he has caused. He refuses to come out of his house and has not eaten for several days. A spokesman for the palace said that David was lying on the floor, pleading with God, and should not be disturbed. (See Psa. 51.)

Tragic news: **Royal baby dies**
There was more bad news for David and Bathsheba today when their baby died after a sudden illness. Both parents are grieving their loss.

Being sorry doesn't always mean that everything turns out OK. God forgave David and their relationship was restored – he even started singing again. But David lost his son and some of his credibility. Disobedience to God causes unnecessary trauma in our lives and can hurt others too. Sort things out with God before a situation gets out of control.

FORGIVEN

'and because the LORD loved him, he sent word … to name him Jedidiah.'

2 Samuel 12:25

David has **ADMITTED HIS MISTAKES** and suffered for his foolishness. He has started to strum his harp with a few heavy numbers about his experience. Does David have any doubts that God has forgiven him?

David might have expected God to kick him out of His family and slam the door in his face. He desperately wanted to put things right with God – but would 'sorry' be enough? David discovered that **GOD WAS PREPARED TO FORGIVE HIM** despite the dreadful things he had done. Yes, David had to suffer the consequences of his actions, but his close relationship with God was restored.

The test of God's love came when David and Bathsheba had a second child. If God was carrying any grudges against them then surely this child would suffer too. They named the boy Solomon, which means 'peace'. Perhaps after all the turmoil, David knew he was at peace with God again.

Kings often had two names, one official name and a second 'family' name. Here comes Nathan again. Another guilt-provoking story? No, it's a newsflash from heaven. God wants the child's family name to be 'Jedidiah'.

David and Bathsheba were thrilled – Jedidiah meant 'beloved by the Lord'. There could be no doubt. God had forgiven David – and Bathsheba too!

>ENGAGE

Don't get pulled into a spiral of guilt because you feel that God won't forgive you for something you have done. God promises that if we honestly own up and really want to live for Him, He will always forgive us and remain as our Friend.

PRAY

Lord God, thank You for forgiving me and loving me. Thank You that because of You, I don't have to feel guilty. Amen.

HONESTY

CIVIL WAR

'And Absalom would add, "If only I were appointed judge in the land! Then everyone who has a complaint or case could come to me and I would see that they receive justice." Also, whenever anyone approached him to bow down before him, Absalom would reach out his hand, take hold of him and kiss him. Absalom behaved in this way towards all the Israelites who came to the king asking for justice, and so he stole the hearts of the people of Israel.'

2 Samuel 15:4–6

David is forgiven and knows it, but the knock-on effects of his crimes continue. God had warned that calamity would come to his family. It comes in the shape of one of David's sons, Absalom, who has ambitions to depose his father as king. Absalom goes on a four-year public relations campaign.

He cultivates a Mr Charming-Humble-Nice-Guy image. He craftily rubbishes his father behind his back.

When he thinks he is ahead in the opinion polls, he makes his move. Absalom declares he is king.

David retreats to rally his supporters. Civil war breaks out. Against David's wishes, Absalom is assassinated in battle. ***DAVID REMAINS KING BUT***

GRIEVES THE DEATH OF HIS SON.

Absalom's rebellion shows what happens if we let envy eat away at us. We not only become bitter but stir up trouble that ends in conflict. God doesn't want us to put on a smarmy nice-guy image to impress people. Neither is it right to bad-mouth someone behind their back.

One of the songs David wrote says, 'Rescue me from those who pursue me' (Psa. 142:6), another goes, 'Arise, LORD! Deliver me, my God!' (Psa. 3:7). David knew that it is God who steps into action and rescues us from whatever or whoever we're facing – we don't need to be like Absalom and try to take things into our own hands.

>ENGAGE

Perhaps the most important thing to learn from David is that the best way of dealing with life's problems and pleasures is to take them to God. Is there anyone who is really bugging you at the moment? Ask God to help you forgive them and for Him to intervene in His own way.

DOUBT-BUSTERS

CREDIBILITY

'The life appeared; we have seen it and testify to it, and we proclaim to you the eternal life, which was with the Father and has appeared to us. We proclaim to you what we have seen and heard, so that you also may have fellowship with us. And our fellowship is with the Father and with his Son, Jesus Christ.'

1 John 1:2–3

At a time when most of the great giants of the Early Church were no longer around, John, by then an old man, wrote to the churches. He was concerned about false teachers (gnostics) making out that Jesus was just a really good guy but not the Son of God. These ***CON MERCHANTS*** claimed they had a hotline to heaven that was more up to date than the written Word of God. Their lies, packaged up as hot-from-heaven happenings, were causing all kinds of doubts. John, who had worked closely with Jesus and witnessed His death and resurrection, reacted by putting together a doubt-busting letter we now know as 1 John – exposing the lies and revealing the truth.

John begins 'Doubt-busters volume one' by listing his credentials. As far as new life in Jesus was concerned, he'd been there, done it, read the book and got the T-shirt!

Of all the disciples, he'd been closest to Jesus. He was the ultimate at-the-scene witness to Jesus' miracles. And he'd seen Jesus several times after the resurrection.

However, John's **GREATEST CREDIBILITY** as a doubt-buster wasn't that he'd hung around with Jesus but that his life had been changed by Him.

As a young man, John was a hothead with a short fuse. He'd been nicknamed 'son of thunder'. When the Samaritans snubbed him he wanted God to fry them alive with a fireburst from heaven.

Jesus changed all that. John, filled with the Holy Spirit at Pentecost, had his life stamped with love instead of hate. He developed a deep care and concern for people.

Early Church writings record that John, as a very old man, was carried to church on a stretcher. On entering the building he would sit up and shout his catchphrase, 'Love one another' and repeat it many times during the service.

>ENGAGE

Many people today are agnostics – they're not sure what to make of Jesus, and have doubts about God. If you have doubts, don't be afraid to tell God about them. He'll help you get to the truth, and change your life too. Ask Him to fill you with the Holy Spirit as we look at 'Doubt-busters', so you can be 'tattooed' with God's love!

SELF-DECEPTION DOUBT-BUSTERS

'If we confess our sins, he is faithful and just and will forgive us our sins and purify us from all unrighteousness.' **1 John 1:9**

Let's look at a couple of doubts about sin and forgiveness ...

Lie number 1: You're an OK person and can get on with God without all that 'Jesus' stuff

The con men had conned themselves into thinking they didn't have a sin problem in their lives to sort out and didn't need Jesus to forgive them. John didn't tell them to get a life but to **GET A LIGHT.** Compare yourself to others and you can remain in the dark about your condition. It's only as we compare our lives to God's standards of holiness that the truth comes to light – and we realise we need Jesus to clean us up.

Lie number 2: You're too bad to be forgiven

This old trick keeps resurfacing. And we are most vulnerable when we let God down – badly. We wonder if God will forgive us ... and instead of sorting things out with Him, we can set off on a long and wasted guilt trip.

In response to these, John sends in two giant doubt-busters ...

Truth number 1: 'The blood of Jesus, his Son, purifies us from all sin' (v7)

Repeat ALL SIN ... yep, really ... ALL SIN! The innocent blood of Jesus, shed on the cross, is full payment for our disobedience. His sacrifice cleans up the most dastardly deeds. Never doubt God will forgive you if you genuinely want to stop living your way and live for Him instead.

Truth number 2: Jesus will 'purify us from all unrighteousness' (v9)

Read it for yourself ... ALL unrighteousness! That means there's not an unright thing God can't put right. When God says He forgives us, He means it. However, there is a condition to the promise of forgiveness ... 'if we confess our sins'. We need to come clean with God to get clean with God.

Memorise verses 7 and 9. If you ever doubt God's forgiveness, call in these doubt-busters to put your mind at rest.

PRAY

Father, thank You for forgiving me for absolutely everything I've done wrong. Amen.

GENUINE ARTICLE

'We know that we have come to know him if we keep his commands. Whoever says, "I know him," but does not do what he commands is a liar, and the truth is not in that person. But if anyone obeys his word, love for God is truly made complete in them. This is how we know we are in him: whoever claims to live in him must live as Jesus did. Dear friends, I am not writing you a new command but an old one, which you have had since the beginning. This old command is the message you have heard.' **1 John 2:3–7**

There are loads of people who make out they are speaking the truth about God. How do you tell the **GENUINE ARTICLE** from the fakes? John says the way to tell a fake is by the way they walk. So, is there a Ministry of Silly Walks? No, what John meant is that a true teacher obeys God – a fake doesn't. You don't just talk the talk but you actually walk the walk as well, in other words you live out what you say you believe.

The false teachers all claimed to know God – almost as if they had a satellite link to heaven. They laid on the 'God has told me' act very heavily so people didn't dare to question them – even when their views contradicted what God had written.

The giveaway was in the way they lived. They claimed to know God but they didn't obey Him. They could talk *about* God but they didn't walk *with* God. They might appear to be friendly sheep with lovely woolly messages but underneath they were **WOLVES.**

Here's John's doubt-buster statement: Genuine teachers walk the talk.

Those who speak the truth want to live the truth. They don't rewrite the rules but live by God's laws.

That's a challenge to us too. People will watch our actions to see how genuine we are. Real Christianity is being real for Christ. Ask God to help you walk the talk today.

HUMBLE OR STUMBLE

'Anyone who loves their brother and sister lives in the light, and there is nothing in them to make them stumble. But anyone who hates a brother or sister is in the darkness and walks around in the darkness. They do not know where they are going, because the darkness has blinded them.' **1 John 2:10–11**

John was on the spot when Jesus gave His disciples a new commandment: 'Love each other as I have loved you.' He wrote it down in his Gospel (John 15:12) and it became his catchphrase. John used Jesus' command to detect those really living for God.

A grumbler makes out he's an excellent Christian. But behind the scenes he knocks other Christians with sour comments and malicious gossip. He will never grow to be the Christian he makes himself out to be until he learns to love those in God's family. He only wants to knock others down to build himself up, which will cause him to stumble. ***THOSE WHO LIVE FOR JESUS LEARN TO LOVE LIKE JESUS.***

Verdict: Hatred makes you stumble.

Those who are humble and forgiving don't try to make themselves out to be better than they are. They go out of their way to get alongside other Christians and befriend them. They focus on their good points rather than their bad. They're able to get on with other Christians because they pray for them, especially those who wind them up. They appreciate just how much God has forgiven them and are ready to forgive others when they make mistakes.

Verdict: Love makes you humble.

If you've been holding a grudge against another Christian, be radical and start praying for them. It's better to be humble than to stumble.

Lord Jesus, help me to be humble. Help me to forgive other people, just like You forgive me. Amen.

THE TIME IS NOW

'I write to you, dear children, because you know the Father. I write to you, fathers, because you know him who is from the beginning. I write to you, young men, because you are strong, and the word of God lives in you, and you have overcome the evil one.' **1 John 2:14**

John has some doubt-busting comments for new Christians, young Christians and older Christians.

New Christians

Have you recently become a Christian? John reminds you that you have been **TOTALLY FORGIVEN** because of Jesus. You are a member of God's family and He is your heavenly Father. It's important to get to know Him by reading your Bible, talking with Him in prayer and meeting up with other Christians.

Young Christians

You may hold a Bible, but does the Bible hold you? The young men John was writing to had learnt to resist temptation by learning and obeying God's ways. The Bible didn't live on the shelf but in their lives.

Although they were young Christians, they were strong Christians. It's important not to miss out on a daily intake of strength from God. The Bible is God's great doubt-buster.

Older Christians

John simply states that these older Christians knew Jesus. Yes, they knew Him personally. They'd chatted with Him through good times and bad. They'd found Him to be a great and reliable Friend.

The great thing is, no matter what stage we're at, we all have eternity to look forward to, where we can get to know Jesus even better.

There's no better time to get to know Jesus than now! There's no better time to read the Bible than now! There's no better time to pray ... or praise ... or give thanks ... than ... you've guessed it ... now! So what are you going to do now? Simply start by thanking God for loving you.

I SEE, I WANT

'Do not love the world or anything in the world. If anyone loves the world, love for the Father is not in them. For everything in the world – the lust of the flesh, the lust of the eyes, and the pride of life – comes not from the Father but from the world. The world and its desires pass away, but whoever does the will of God lives for ever.' **1 John 2:15–17**

 John highlights two types of love:

1. Love of this world

We can tell whether we're loving the world more than God if we are becoming 'grabbers, spotters and boasters'.

Grabbers: It's easy to get sidetracked into a lifestyle of get, get, get, rather than give, give, give. We want, want, want ... and then want more. We model ourselves on the **LATEST IMAGE** – forgetting that what's in today is out tomorrow.

Spotters: Our eyes can put our lives out of focus. **WE SEE SOMETHING – WE WANT IT.** And that can apply to people too. Do you find that your eyes automatically start tracking fanciable members of the opposite sex? If we are to let God influence our thoughts and actions, we must let Him influence what or who we watch.

Boasters: Why do we fall in love with things? The more we have, the more flash we can appear. It might impress some but not God. He knows what's really going on in our lives.

2. Love of God

Those who **PUT GOD FIRST** live to give. God, not the world, shapes their attitudes and lifestyle. Those who put God first, watch that they honour Him in their relationships. Those who put God first live to please Him. It's not what 'I want' but what God wants that counts.

Ask God to help you get your priorities sorted today.

PRIORITISE

LITMUS TEST

'I do not write to you because you do not know the truth, but because you do know it and because no lie comes from the truth. Who is the liar? It is whoever denies that Jesus is the Christ. Such a person is the antichrist – denying the Father and the Son. No one who denies the Son has the Father; whoever acknowledges the Son has the Father also.' **1 John 2:21–23**

Many people say they believe in God and some may try to persuade you to go along with their ideas. So how do you suss out who's right and wrong? One big clue is what they make of Jesus.

Against Christ

To be anti-Jesus is not necessarily to say nasty things about Him. It's denying that He's God's Son. Some say that Jesus was a great man, top-notch prophet, ace revolutionary ... but ask them whether they think Jesus is God's Son, who died to save us from sin and rose to life, and they start to dodge the issue. John doesn't mince his words – if you don't believe Jesus is God's Son then you are against Jesus!

A good test as to whether someone is telling the truth about God is to ask whether they believe in God the Father, God the Son (Jesus) and God the Holy Spirit. Most false teaching will deny one or more Persons of the Trinity.

For Christ

Those who know the truth speak the truth about Jesus. They don't size Him down to being a good man – they worship Him as their Saviour and Lord. Each generation in history has had those who are against Christ (usually the majority) and those who are for Him. John announces in the book of Revelation that sometime in the future a powerful person will emerge with the title Anti-Christ who will be extremely hostile to Jesus and His followers. **JESUS WILL SORT HIM OUT!** No sweat. He's God's Son with greater power than Satan! Praise Him!

God says that one day everyone, including those who are against Jesus, will bow down and recognise that Jesus Christ is Lord. Why wait? Tell Jesus you're for Him now!

THEY THINK IT'S ALL OVER ...

'As for you, see that what you have heard from the beginning remains in you. If it does, you also will remain in the Son and in the Father. And this is what he promised us – eternal life.' **1 John 2:24–25**

What happens when you die? Some will tell you that's it – it's all over; heaven is fantasy land. Others think you come back to life as a different person. John comes up with a big doubt-buster statement on the matter.

God promises **ETERNAL LIFE** to those who believe in Jesus (v25)! Death is not the end. So don't let anyone mislead you into thinking it is. Neither is there some kind of waiting room where you are punished for your wrongs on earth and eventually let into heaven when you have served your sentence. The Bible is very clear that those who trust in Jesus have eternal life right away and those who don't trust Jesus will never make heaven.

As for re-emerging as a different person or animal in another era – forget it. That's not what God says. It's a lie. You are a unique person with **ONE LIFETIME** to make up your mind about God. John's advice is to trust in Jesus. Hold on to what the Bible says about the future. Other theories are counterfeit.

John also reminds us that Jesus promises to return. Suppose it was today. What would you say? 'Whoops, sorry about the mess Lord – if I'd known you were coming I'd have tidied up my life.' Or would He catch you doing something good? John's advice is to keep our lives in order so we won't be embarrassed should Jesus return today.

>ENGAGE

Eternal life is the most valuable gift in the world – and it comes free from God (with the Holy Spirit as the guarantee) to those who trust Jesus to save them. Don't doubt it! You can be confident God will keep His promise. Tell Him how this makes you feel, and most of all – thank Him!

ETERNITY

SONS OF GOD

'See what great love the Father has lavished on us, that we should be called children of God! And that is what we are! The reason the world does not know us is that it did not know him. Dear friends, now we are children of God, and what we will be has not yet been made known. But we know that when Christ appears, we shall be like him, for we shall see him as he is. All who have this hope in him purify themselves, just as he is pure.'

1 John 3:1–3

Have you ever felt God doesn't care about you? Or doubted whether you are really part of His family? Here's a couple of doubt-busters to zap your fears.

God has a great love for you!

John gets excited when he talks about God's love. And it's not a one-off show of care when we become a Christian. God lavishes His love on us. That means He keeps dishing it out in huge quantities – even when we've been disobedient. Our love for God may run hot and cold but ***HIS LOVE FOR US NEVER CHANGES.***

You are a child of God

John is gobsmacked to think he's part of God's family. Wow! He knows he doesn't deserve to be. However, God's love is so incredible that those who trust Jesus are not only forgiven but made children of God.

Yes, that's what we are! Can you believe that? We have a loving heavenly Father who cares about us. John goes on to remind us that one day we will see Him. All our fears will be a thing of the past and we will live with Him forever.

Even as an old man, John marvelled at the privilege of being a child of God. And we should be thankful to God for His care too. John suggests a great way for us to show our gratitude – by living pure lives (v3). Obedience speaks louder than words.

Lord God, thank You for loving me. Help me to live in a way that shows You I'm grateful. Amen.

THE U-TURN

'The one who does what is sinful is of the devil, because the devil has been sinning from the beginning. The reason the Son of God appeared was to destroy the devil's work. No one who is born of God will continue to sin, because God's seed remains in them; they cannot go on sinning, because they have been born of God. This is how we know who the children of God are and who the children of the devil are: anyone who does not do what is right is not God's child, nor is anyone who does not love their brother and sister.' **1 John 3:8–10**

A bunch of con-men teachers were telling Christians that as long as they believed the right things, how they behaved wasn't important. They thought that breaking God's rules with their bodies didn't matter as God would save their souls. John sorts them out and sets things straight.

Genuine Christians want to live by God's rules

When you become a Christian there is a U-turn in your life. You turn away from the things that displease God and you turn to live His way instead. Unfortunately, that's not as easy as it sounds, as our old selfish nature likes to have the final say.

So how do you tell the **GENUINE CHRISTIAN** from the fake – when they both fail God. The fake won't care what God thinks and will continue to be deliberately disobedient. John warns that those who claim to be Christians but continue to break God's rules may not be Christians at all. The genuine child of God will want to say sorry and not repeat his mistakes. He'll want to get right with God and live right for God ... and won't be happy until he does.

When God rules in your life, God's rules are important. A disobedient child of God is still a child of God, but has things to sort out with his heavenly Father. If that sounds like you, why not get back on the right track now?

RIGHT TRACK

BROTHER VERSUS BROTHER

'For this is the message you heard from the beginning: we should love one another. Do not be like Cain, who belonged to the evil one and murdered his brother. And why did he murder him? Because his own actions were evil and his brother's were righteous. Do not be surprised, my brothers and sisters, if the world hates you. We know that we have passed from death to life, because we love each other. Anyone who does not love remains in death.' **1 John 3:11**

Halfway through his letter, John decides to repeat his catchphrase – just in case we missed it first time round: 'love one another'!

So where did Cain go wrong (see Gen. 4:1–8)?

- He wasn't able to control his anger
- He became consumed with jealousy
- He had bitterness written on his face
- He refused to sort himself out – God's way
- He ignored God's warnings that his hatred was getting out of control
- He murdered Abel

A spark of jealousy lit a flame of bitterness that turned into an inferno of hatred – then murder. John uses this brother versus brother murder case to remind us not to hold grudges against others.

GOD'S WAY is to show love, not hatred – especially to other Christians. A so-called harmless bit of gossip can soon develop into a character assassination and a murdered reputation. Things can get out of hand very quickly and the hurt can last a lifetime. John, after all, had found it hard to control his anger and rage as a young man.

So John repeats his catchphrase: 'We should love one another.'

Do people know you are a Christian because of the caring way you treat people? Jesus said that we should be noticed for our love. Ask God to fill you with the Holy Spirit so you can love others today.

ROLL UP YOUR SLEEVES

'This is how we know what love is: Jesus Christ laid down his life for us. And we ought to lay down our lives for our brothers and sisters. If anyone has material possessions and sees a brother or sister in need but has no pity on them, how can the love of God be in that person?' **1 John 3:16–17**

Do you think John's catchphrase, 'Love one another' sounds a bit wishy-washy, lovey-dovey? Does it conjure up images of Christians in sandals and socks, hugging each other, saying things like 'flower power' and generally being a bit wimpy? John goes on to explain what his catchphrase really means.

John certainly wasn't a lovey-dovey type of bloke. He was a **ROUGH, TOUGH, WORKING MAN WITH A QUICK TEMPER.** You didn't mess with him. He was a down-to-earth man who showed God's love by rolling up his sleeves and helping those in need. John saw God's love in action in the life of Jesus. Jesus fed the hungry, befriended the lonely and helped the poor. While Jesus was dying on the cross, it was John who comforted Mary. He put her up at his house and made sure she was properly fed and looked after.

John's advice to us is this: if you want to know what 'Love one another' means – copy Jesus. He gave up everything to help us. He gave until it hurt and when it hurt He kept giving. The follow-on is this: if someone is in need and you can help, **GET INTO ACTION RIGHT AWAY.** Be practical, be real, be a friend.

>ENGAGE

When Peter and John saw a lame man begging outside the Temple, they stopped to help him. God's love was backed up with God's power and a moment later the lame man was dancing around praising God. Often the best way to show God's love is not to preach out, but to reach out to those in need.

PRAY

God, I want to show people that You love them, not just tell them. Please show me how to do that! Amen.

FACTS, NOT FEELINGS

'And this is his command: to believe in the name of his Son, Jesus Christ, and to love one another as he commanded us. The one who keeps God's commands lives in him, and he in them. And this is how we know that he lives in us: we know it by the Spirit he gave us.'

1 John 3:23–24

It's not only people who can seriously try to con us – our feelings can too. Have you ever felt down for no particular reason – you don't have that Christian feel-good factor and doubt whether you're much of a Christian at all? Most Christians feel like that from time to time.

John announces another doubt-buster to help us. Rely on the facts, not your feelings.

Our feelings can go up and down like a yo-yo, but **GOD'S PROMISES DON'T CHANGE.** God is greater than our feelings and the things that get to us.

John lists some commands of God to test against ourselves.

1: Do you believe in Jesus Christ, God's Son?

If you have, then the fact is that you are forgiven and are a member of God's family – whether you feel like it or not.

2: Are you obeying His commands?

Sometimes the reason we can feel low is that we've gone **OFF THE RAILS.** The Holy Spirit is not filling our lives but is sad at our indifference. It's a prompt to get right with God again. However, it's possible to be forgiven and still feel low. John says we can be confident that God has made us clean – don't let your feelings mislead you. Of course, there may be many other reasons for feeling down. Don't be afraid to express your feelings to God and ask Him to put your mind at rest.

3: Are you loving one another?

John couldn't resist bringing up his catchphrase again. If we are at peace with God and at peace with others, then we can be at peace with ourselves.

Let's face the facts: God loves you. Jesus died for you. You've been chosen; you're special. And what's more, you're going to spend eternity with God – and that's a fact!

Father God, thank You that however I feel, the facts still tell me that You love me. Let those facts stick in my head and my heart. Amen.

WISHFUL THINKING

'This is how you can recognise the Spirit of God: every spirit that acknowledges that Jesus Christ has come in the flesh is from God, but every spirit that does not acknowledge Jesus is not from God. This is the spirit of the antichrist, which you have heard is coming and even now is already in the world.' **1 John 4:2–3**

Not everyone who says God has told them this or that is speaking the truth. For some it might be wishful thinking. There are some misled by devious evil spirits who dress up the results as coming from God. How can you tell the false prophet from the real thing?

John has a doubt-buster test that separates those who have heard from God from those who are being misled. His advice is: **FIND OUT WHAT THEY MAKE OF JESUS.**

It's very simple. If they don't believe Jesus is God's one and only Son, then their message isn't from God.

Satan hates to concede that Jesus is God's Son, who came as a man to die for our sins. There's a good reason for that – when Jesus rose from the dead, He made a way for people to escape from death to eternal life. And Satan is powerless to stop it. It infuriates him to see Christians worshipping Jesus as their Saviour and Lord.

Satan is a loser on a damage limitation exercise, persuading people to reject or ignore Jesus. The last thing he wants is for Jesus to be known for who He is – God's Son. So John's test is a good one. Those with a false view about Jesus don't speak for God.

In 1820, Joseph Smith claimed to have had visions from God and founded the Mormon church. When we apply John's test, we discover the Mormons call Jesus 'the Son' but don't believe He's God's one and only Son. Verdict: False!

In the 1870s, Charles Russell founded the Jehovah's Witnesses. They'll knock on your door claiming to speak for God. When we apply John's test, we discover they don't believe Jesus is the Son of God but a created being. Verdict: False!

Why not declare the truth (loudly!)? Praise God for Jesus, His one and only Son, who died and rose again so we could be forgiven. Hallelujah! Go on, try it now!

HOW QUICKLY WE FORGET

'Dear children, let us not love with words or speech but with actions and in truth. This is how we know that we belong to the truth and how we set our hearts at rest in his presence: if our hearts condemn us, we know that God is greater than our hearts, and he knows everything.' **1 John 3:18–20**

John is a great doubt-busting teacher. He knows how quickly we forget. So he keeps repeating his catchphrase. What have we got to do? Love each other! You can do better than that. Let's hear it again ... LOVE each other!

John has another test to separate those who know God from those who don't. God is love ... 100% love ... that's His character. And those who know God are learning to show the same love.

If you have any doubts that God loves you, just look at the facts:

- We were cut off from God due to our independence.
- God is holy and the penalty for sin must be met.
- God takes action to **BREAK THE DEADLOCK.**

- His innocent Son, Jesus, is sent to earth as a sacrifice.
- Jesus willingly takes the death penalty we deserve.
- Those who trust in Jesus are made right with God.

Now if God's done all that for us – we should show the same love to others. It's not a love we can put on with a bit of smarm and charm. God gives us the Holy Spirit, and as we learn to let the Holy Spirit guide our lives, the more caring we become. Let's hear it again ... Love each other. Just as God loves us.

>ENGAGE

OK, OK, John. That's the third time you reminded us about loving other Christians. Or, maybe it's a message we need to hear again ...

PRAY

Lord Jesus, I get the point John is making! I know I need to love other Christians. But sometimes I struggle to. Please help me to do that. Amen.

JESUS IN THE SPOTLIGHT

'This is how we know that we live in him and he in us: he has given us of his Spirit. And we have seen and testify that the Father has sent his Son to be the Saviour of the world. If anyone acknowledges that Jesus is the Son of God, God lives in them and they in God.' **1 John 4:13–15**

John has another test of the true Christian. How do you know you really belong to God?

Fasten your seatbelts! John revs up with another doubt-buster statement: Those who **BELONG TO GOD** have the Holy Spirit in their lives. John knew this from experience. He'd heard Jesus promise to send the Holy Spirit (John 16:5–16). After the resurrection, he'd waited in Jerusalem on Jesus' orders for the arrival of the Holy Spirit. On the day of Pentecost, John and those praying together were filled with the Holy Spirit. Immediately they were up and doing the things God wanted them to do.

Jesus also told John that the Holy Spirit would show them the truth. They preached that Jesus is God's Son. True! That God had raised Jesus to life. True! That we need to turn to Jesus for forgiveness. True!

Jesus had told John that the Holy Spirit would put the spotlight on Him. That's what happened. Three thousand people believed in Jesus that day.

It was the Holy Spirit who changed John's hot head into a warm heart.

>ENGAGE

When you believe in Jesus, not only are you made clean but also you receive the Holy Spirit into your life. People's experiences of receiving the Holy Spirit vary a lot. For some it is very dramatic and for others low-key. It's important that we take John's advice and rely on the facts, not our feelings. However, the fact we have the Holy Spirit doesn't mean He's in control of our lives. We can limit His influence by continuing to be selfish. It's vital, if we are to put God's love into action, that we are filled with the Holy Spirit. That's not a one-off experience. We need to come to God each day so He can clean out the junk and top us up with His love.

NO FEAR

'If anyone acknowledges that Jesus is the Son of God, God lives in them and they in God. And so we know and rely on the love God has for us. God is love. Whoever lives in love lives in God, and God in them. This is how love is made complete among us so that we will have confidence on the day of judgment: in this world we are like Jesus. There is no fear in love. But perfect love drives out fear, because fear has to do with punishment.' **1 John 4:15–18**

Fear is a powerful enemy that likes to hijack our minds! It causes us to have doubts about God, doubts about ourselves and doubts about the future.

Here's a doubt-buster to help those who are feeling worried or afraid. Those who know Jesus, who believe and trust in Him, have ***NO REASON TO FEAR DEATH,*** or doubt that they will make it to heaven. If you truly believe in Jesus, there is absolutely no need to be afraid.

GOD'S LOVE DRIVES OUT FEAR. Often we focus on our problems rather than focusing on God's care, and we put ourselves through a lot of unnecessary worry. We fail to appreciate that God's looking after us and is working things out for our good.

John says we have no need to fear God's judgment. God's not going to bring up a long list of our failings. Those who are forgiven have their sins erased, not because they deserve it but because Jesus has met their punishment in full. So there's nothing to worry about – God's love rules and there's nothing that can overpower it.

>ENGAGE

God's love is so powerful it zaps our worries and bulldozes our fears. So if you are fretting about anything, tell Him about it. Remember just how much He cares for you. Remember that God is love. Remember that He is in control. Verdict: 'So we say with confidence, "The Lord is my helper; I will not be afraid"' (Heb. 13:6).

NO CHORE

'This is how we know that we love the children of God: by loving God and carrying out his commands. In fact, this is love for God: to keep his commands. And his commands are not burdensome, for everyone born of God overcomes the world. This is the victory that has overcome the world, even our faith. Who is it that overcomes the world? Only the one who believes that Jesus is the Son of God.' **1 John 5:2–5**

John won't change the subject. Just when you thought it was safe to go moaning about Christians again, he pops up with another reminder about loving each other. John has a way to test our love for God and others. Those who love their fellow Christians, love God.

THOSE WHO LOVE GOD, FOLLOW GOD.

John didn't dream this one up. It was what Jesus had taught him. John knew that Jesus loved God, not because He said so, but because He did what God said – even when it was difficult. The way Jesus put it was this: 'Whoever has my commands and keeps them, is the one who loves me' (John 14:21).

Obey God. Does that sound like a bit of a drag? Boring? Dull? Heavy? Prepare for another doubt-buster.

Obeying God isn't a chore but the best way to live! Putting God first isn't tiresome but sets you free to enjoy life.

Take a look at God's commandments. Can you name one that is a burden? Are any not good for you? So what's the problem? Sometimes the problem is us. Deep down we don't like the idea of going along with God's plans. We'd rather do our own thing than co-operate with our Maker. But by kicking out at God's rules, we open the door to selfishness.

Following God isn't a chore but a great way to live! The best way to live! Here's one of the commands Jesus gave John to put into practice: 'Love each other' (John 15:17).

Now haven't we heard that somewhere before?

Sometimes, loving other people can be very hard, and obeying God can seem almost impossible. However, don't give up: look to Jesus, ask Him for the strength to love and obey – after all, that's God's way.

THE VERDICT

'Whoever believes in the Son of God accepts this testimony. Whoever does not believe God has made him out to be a liar, because they have not believed the testimony God has given about his Son. And this is the testimony: God has given us eternal life, and this life is in his Son. Whoever has the Son has life; whoever does not have the Son of God does not have life.' **1 John 5:10–12**

Some claim that there are many routes into heaven and that it doesn't matter what you believe as long as you are sincere. Is that right?

Lots of ways? No way! One way? Yes. Those who trust Jesus have eternal life. Those without Jesus don't make it. Jesus is the only way we can be made fit for heaven. John leaves us in no doubt about the truth.

Call the first witness: Blood. Question: Are there many ways to God?

No. Sin carries the death sentence. You can't wriggle out of it by trying to act good. Someone has to take the punishment. Jesus died so that we could be forgiven. His innocent blood is the only price God will accept for our entry to heaven.

Call in the next witness: Water. Question: Are there many ways to God?

No. God is holy – 100% pure. And only those who are totally clean can join His family. Sadly we can't clean ourselves up by doing all the churchy nice guy routines. Only Jesus can take away our sin and make us squeaky clean.

Call in the last witness: Holy Spirit. Question: Are there many ways to God?

I speak the truth, the whole truth and nothing but the truth. I testify that **JESUS IS THE ONLY WAY TO GOD.**

What's your verdict? Why not give thanks to God for Jesus, right now? He is the way, and the truth, and the life.

PRAY

God, thank You for sending Jesus to show me the way to You. Tell me the truth about who You are, and give me life. Amen.

DON'T TAKE IT FOR GRANTED

'I write these things to you who believe in the name of the Son of God so that you may know that you have eternal life. This is the confidence we have in approaching God: that if we ask anything according to his will, he hears us. And if we know that he hears us – whatever we ask – we know that we have what we asked of him.' **1 John 5:13–15**

Why did John bother to write all these doubt-busters? He thought it was important to remind people of the truth. That applies to the people of his time who he was writing to directly, and it also applies to all of us today.

The Gospel of John

Here's the reason John gave for writing his Gospel:

'that you may believe that Jesus is the Messiah, the Son of God, and that by believing you may have life in his name' (John 20:31).

John wanted people to study the evidence and discover the truth.

John's letters

John then wrote to encourage those who 'believed in the name of the Son of God'. And he lists some of the benefits of being a Christian – just in case they'd forgotten.

1. Eternal life. Yes, it's for real.
2. You can talk direct to God about anything at any time. He'll listen!
3. God will answer your prayers – in the best possible way and at the best possible time. **BE PATIENT.**

It's so easy to take Jesus and all He's done for granted. Rather than make your prayers a wish list, ask God to show you what He wants for you, and thank Him for sending His Son to save you.

>ENGAGE

In John's other letters, 2 and 3 John, he writes to encourage individuals. They are short letters because he intends to visit them to chat more about Jesus. Is there someone you can encourage by writing to them? Or better still, meet up with and chat? Both are practical ways to show God's love.

NO DIVIDE

'Why do you look at the speck of sawdust in your brother's eye and pay no attention to the plank in your own eye? ... If you see any brother or sister commit a sin that does not lead to death, you should pray and God will give them life.' **Matthew 7:3; 1 John 5:16**

John rounds up his list of doubt-busters with a challenge to get alongside Christians who are out-of-sorts with God.

How should we react when a Christian breaks God's rules – and may not seem to care about it? Here are some guidelines:

1. Don't criticise!

Remember, it could just as easily be you. If we start to point out all the flaws in everyone else, we could end up ignoring the things we need to put right in our own lives.

2. Continue to love that person and show them understanding

Don't reject someone or make them feel like an outcast because of what they have done. We have all done things we're not proud of at one time or another, so we know we need people around us to support us through thick and thin, not abandon us at the first sign we've gone off the tracks.

3. Pray for them and keep on praying

It's easy to judge those who get it wrong. God's way isn't to talk about them behind their back – but to His face. Are there Christians you ought to be praying for now? **GOD HAS PROMISED TO ANSWER.**

4. Remember John's catchphrase: 'Love each other'

Love doesn't set out to divide, but to bring together. Love doesn't keep a list of failings, but shows forgiveness. That's why we need to love each other, just as Christ loves us.

Will you ever be able to forget John's catchphrase? It's worth remembering for life. But, just in case you missed it, John sneaks it in one more time – as the last sentence in the Bible! Turn to Revelation (another book John wrote) chapter 22, verse 21. 'The grace [love] of the Lord Jesus be with God's people. Amen.' God has the final say: 'Love each other!'

PRAY

Lord Jesus, You gave us an example of what it means to love people. Help me to love other people like You do. Amen.

YP's
MAY/JUN 2016
YOUR TIME IS NOW!
GET GOING WITH ELISHA!
CAUGHT IN THE ACTS!
>> Exclusive stories on the Early Church
PITCH UP HERE!
>> What is God's tent all about?
FOR DAILY BIBLE READING
CWR
YP's
MAR/APR 2016
PLUS! QUIZZES, PUZZLES AND YP'S READERS' PAGES!
KNOW WHO YOU ARE
FOR DAILY BIBLE READING
CWR
YP's
JAN/FEB 2016
WHEN THINGS GET TOUGH
JESUS IN TOWN!
>> What happens when Jesus turns up?
YOUR CHOICE!
>> Wise decisions, attitudes and words!
QUIZZES, PUZZLES AND YP'S READERS' PAGES!
FOR DAILY BIBLE READING
CWR

Who is God?
How did we get where we are today?
What is church?
How can I know and live for God?
GUIDE TO
KNOWING
GOD
Jonathan Brant